The Letter Xx

Things I Can See

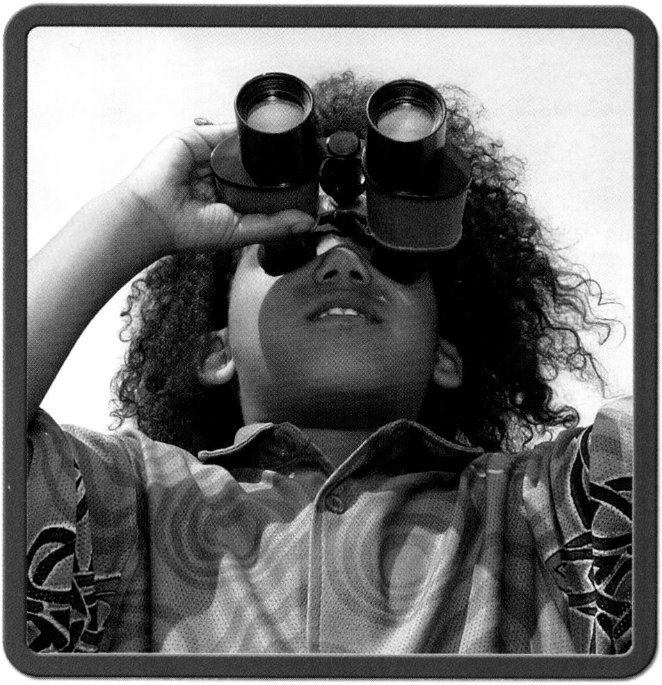

by Hollie J. Endres

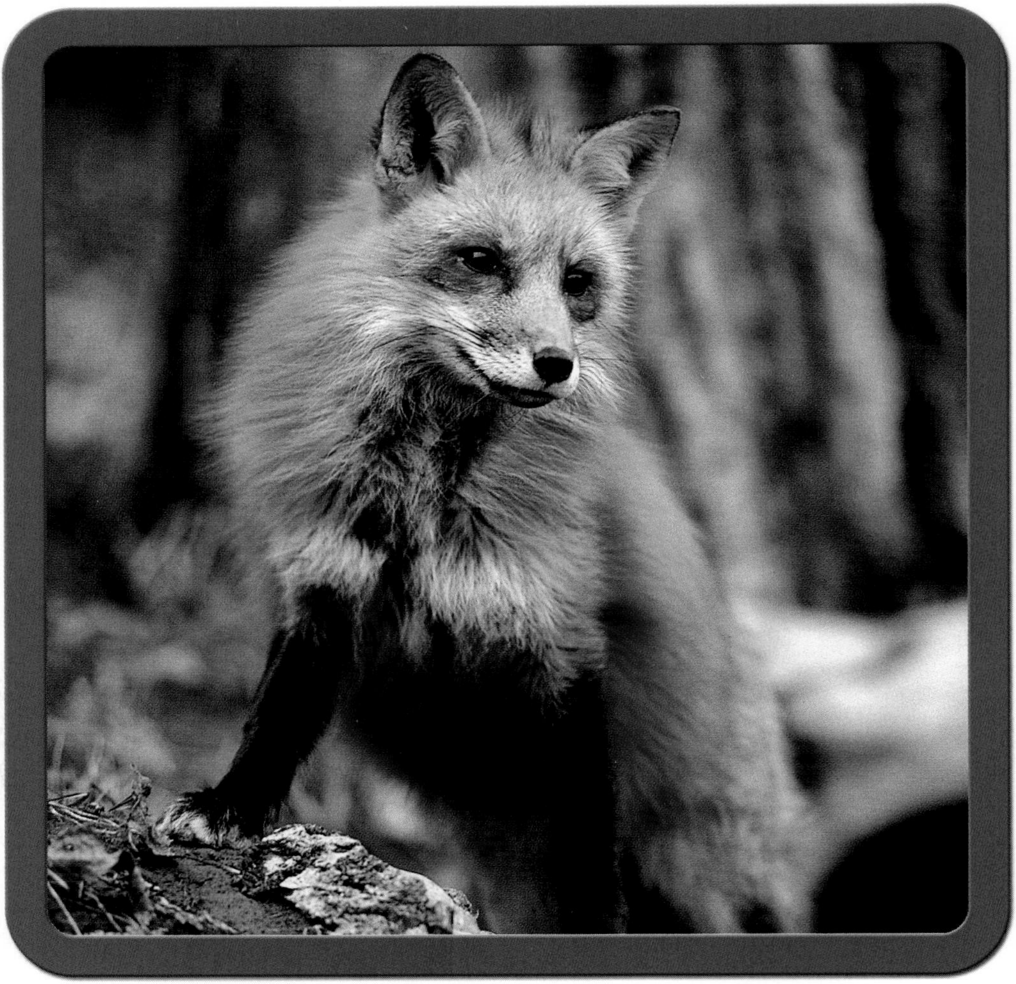

I see a fo**x**.

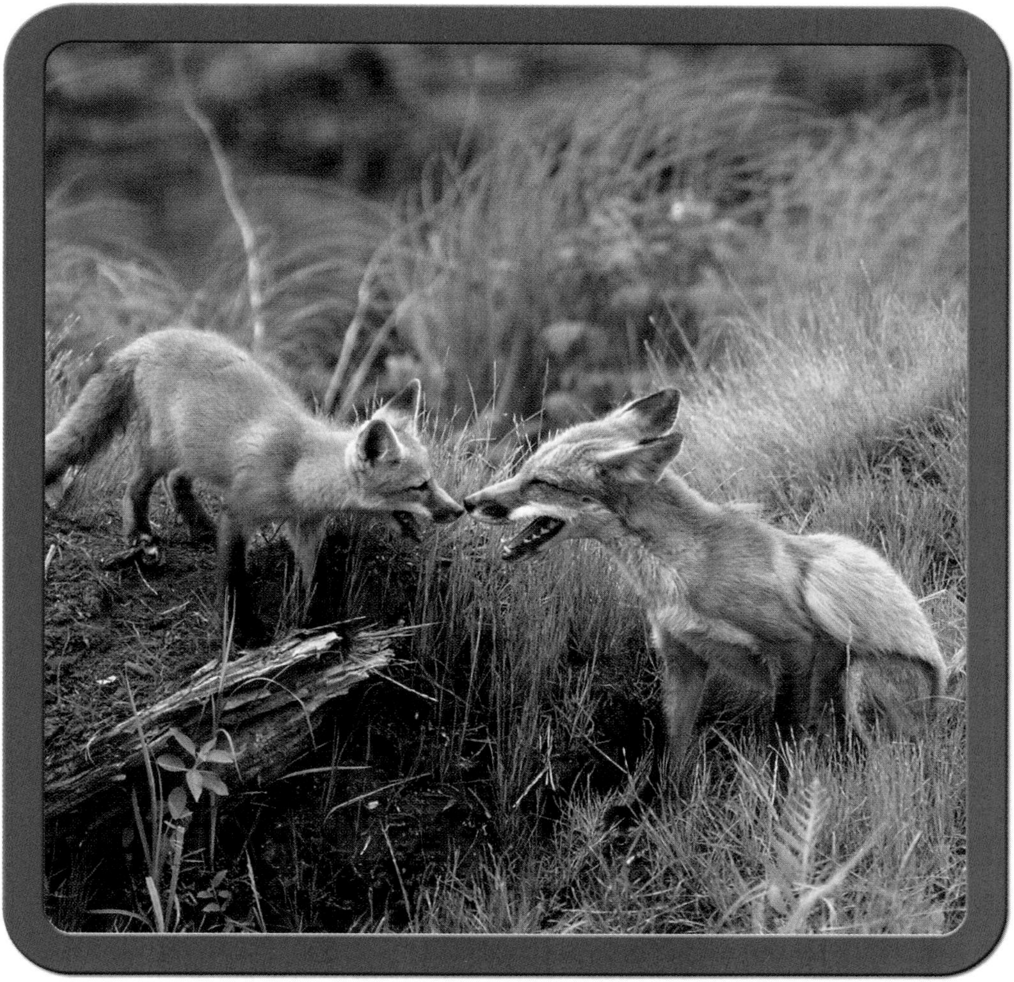

How many can you see?

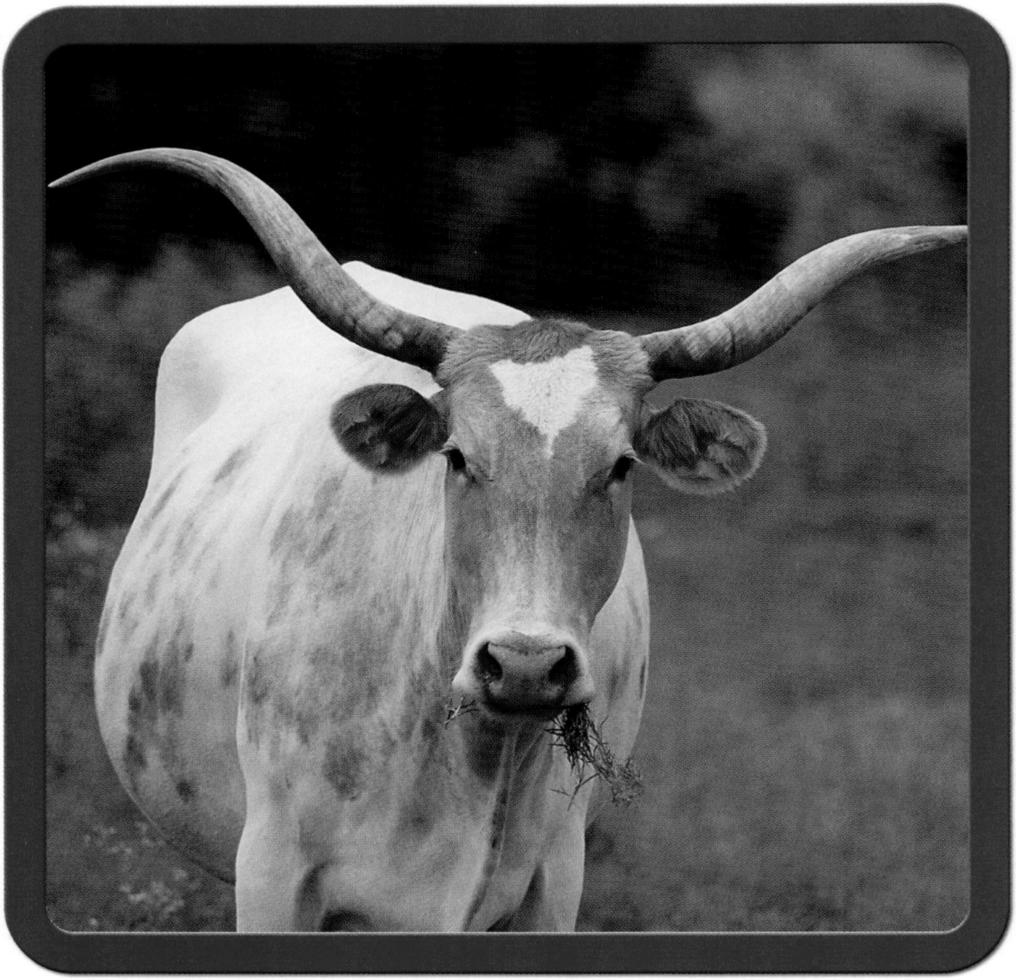

I see an o**x**.

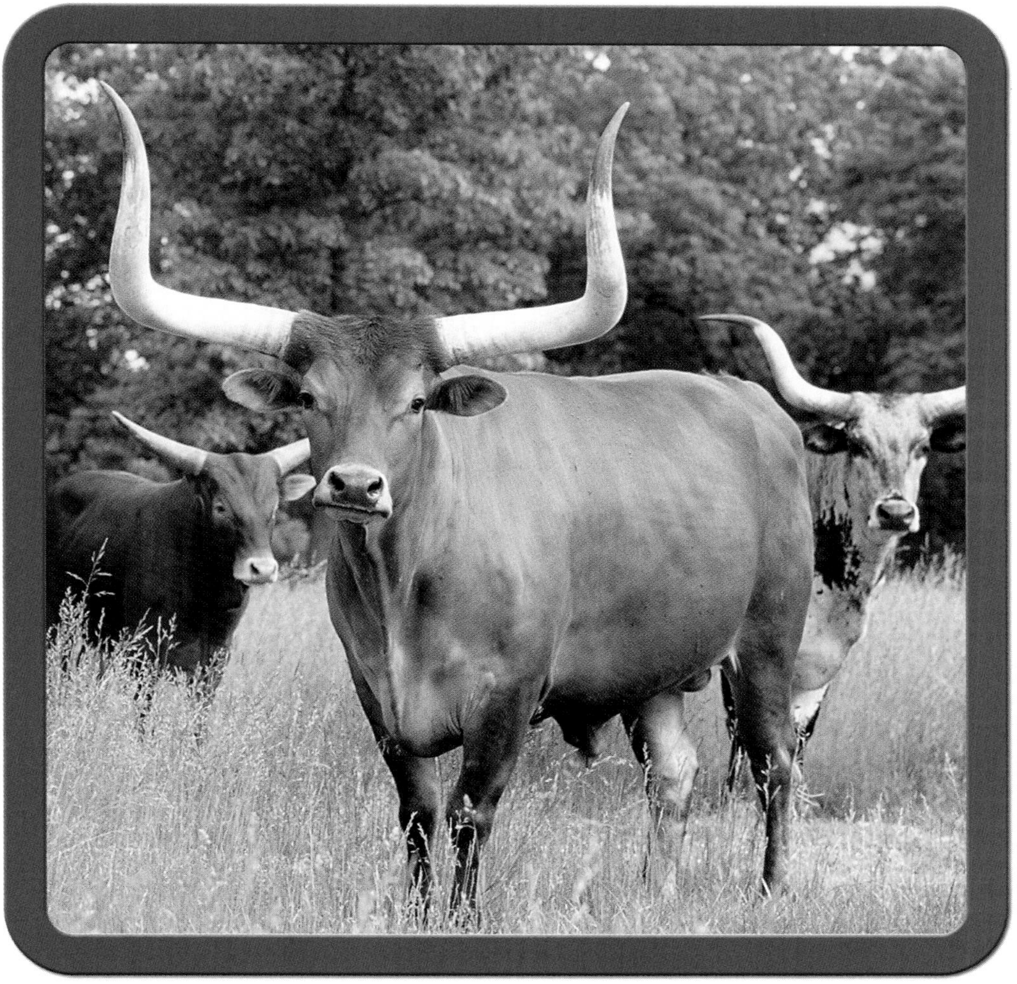

How many can you see?

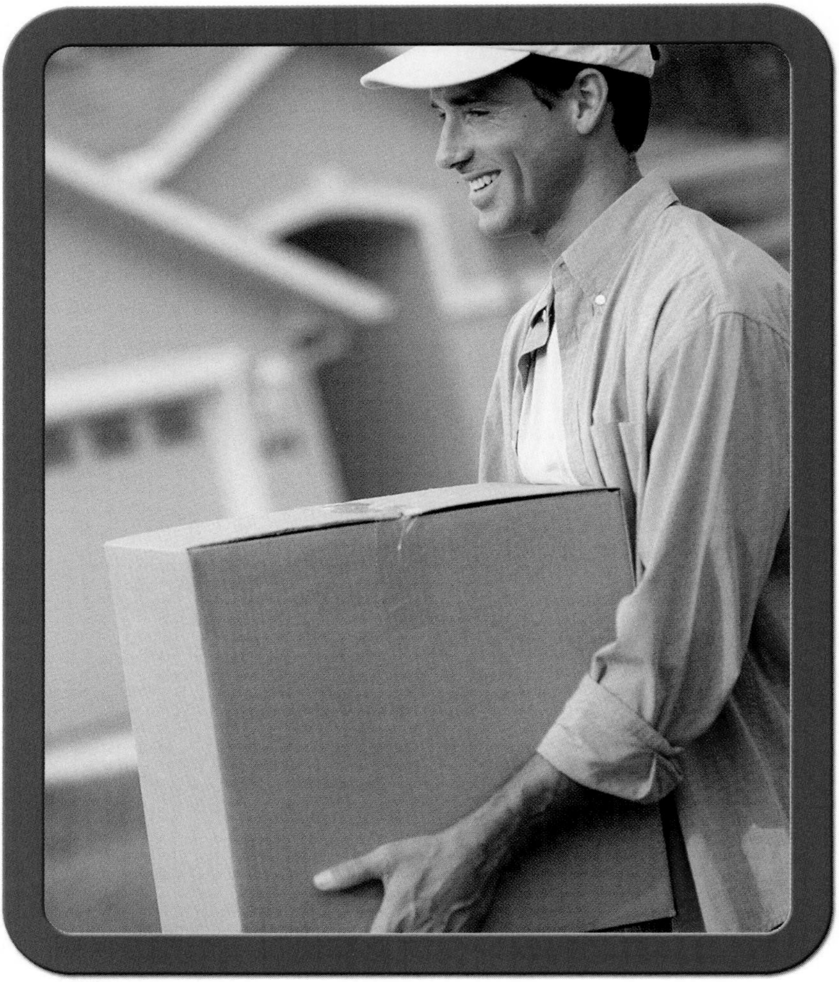

I see a bo**x**.

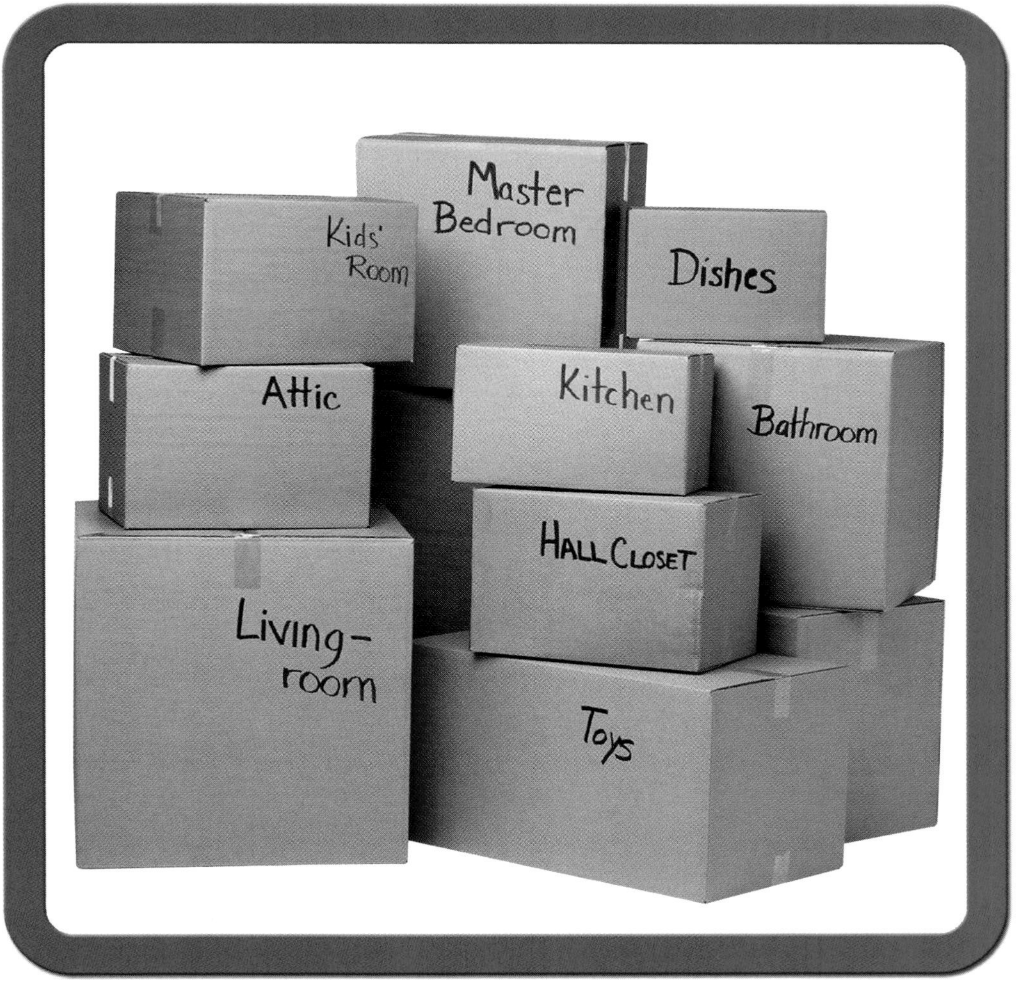

How many can you see?

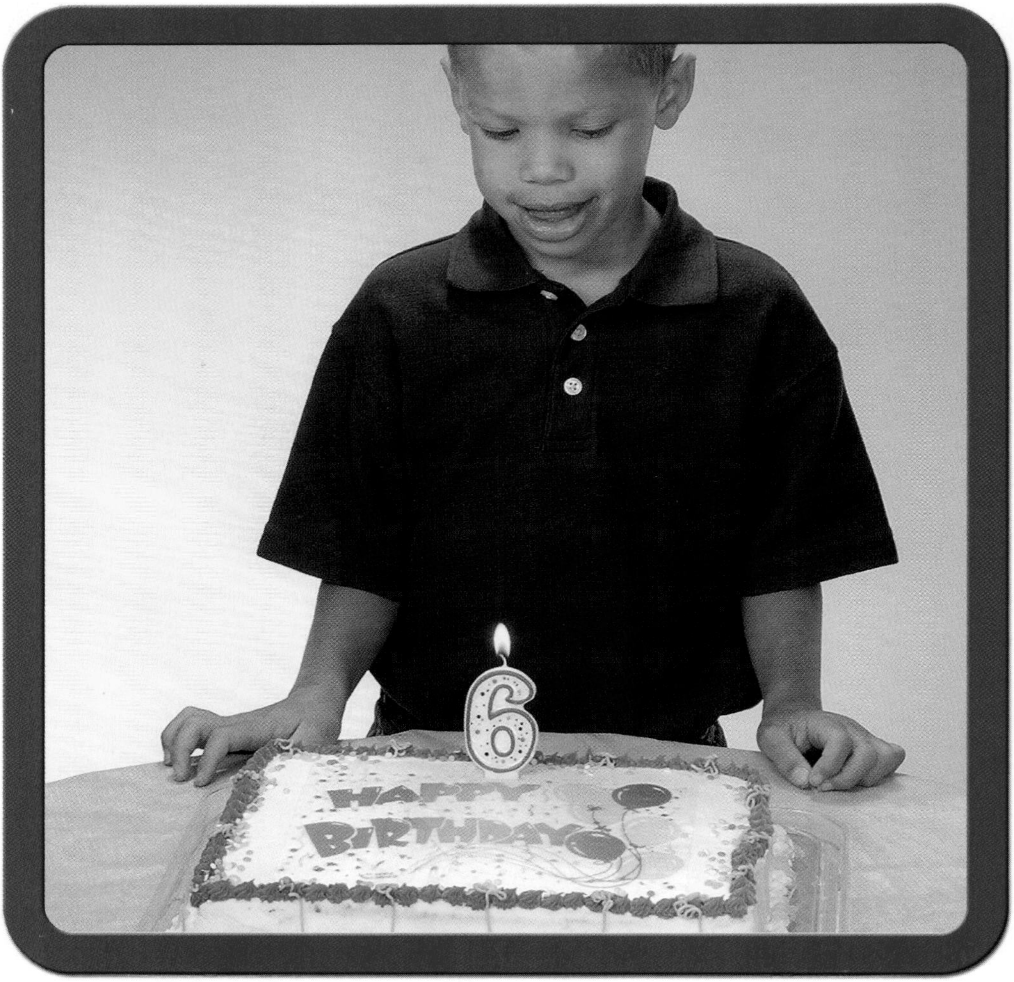
HAPPY
BIRTHDAY

I see a si**x**!